ATLASIA KIDS

Ramadan Journal 2025

Atlasia Team
Editor-in-Chief: Hasan Ahmet Gokce, MA, MEd, PhD
Senior Editor: Sumeyra Ozcan, BA, BLib, MPub
Associate Editors: Zainab Sana Noor, Betul Ozkisi, Sarah Bayza, Jasmine Baten
Educational Consultant: Emma Malik, MEd
Copy Editor: Maya Salem
Graphic Design: BAY Design
Rights and Permissions: Ahmed Guray
Social Media: Safiyya Jeenah
Digital and Audio Production: Gurhan Gulcan

Published by Tughra Books

335 Clifton Ave
Clifton, NJ 07011
www.tughrabooks.com

ISBN 9781597849630

For subscriptions to Atlasia Kids:
www.atlasiakids.com
info@atlasiakids.com

Printed in Canada

As Salaam Alaikum!

Welcome to a journey of discovery and growth with your Atlasia Ramadan Journal. This Ramadan, we invite you to explore the deep lessons and timeless wisdom of this holy month. Your journal is not just a collection of pages; it's a treasure trove of learning, reflection, and creativity. Each day, you'll discover a new hadith, delve into the virtues of our beloved Prophet, and reflect on the days of Ramadan from the Age of Bliss.

Your journal is also a canvas for your thoughts and gratitude, a place to record your Ramadan experiences. Engage in exciting activities on the odd-numbered pages, where fun awaits in the form of puzzles, recipes, crafts, and family games.

As you fast, pray, and read during this holy month, let this journal be your companion. It's a guide to help you appreciate the beauty of Ramadan, understand its teachings, and practice kindness every day. We hope that by the end of Ramadan, your journal will be a colorful reflection of your journey – filled with learnings, reflections, and happy memories.

Let's take this remarkable journey together and make this Ramadan a season to grow, enjoy, and renew spiritually.

Ramadan Mubarak!

Atlasia Team

Stick a picture of you!

THIS JOURNAL BELONGS TO

....

RAMADAN DUAS

Dua for breaking fast

اللَّهُمَّ اِنِّى لَكَ صُمْتُ وَبِكَ
امنْتُ [وَعَلَيْكَ تَوَكَّلْتُ] وَعَلَى
رِزْقِكَ اَفْطَرْتُ

O Allah! I fasted for You, and I believe in You, and I put my trust in You. I break my fast with Your sustenance.

Dua for the family that invites you to break your fast with them

اَفْطَرَ عِنْدَكُم الصّائِمونَ وَأَكَلَ
طَعامَكُمُ الأبْرار، وَصَلَّتْ
عَلَيْكُمُ الملائِكَة

With you, those who are fasting have broken their fast, you have fed those who are righteous, and the angels recite their prayers upon you.

Dua for your parents

رَّبِّ ارْحَمْهُمَا كَمَا رَبَّيَانِي صَغِيرًا

My Lord, have mercy upon them as they brought me up [when I was] small.

Dua for increasing your iman

اَللّٰهُمَّ مُصَرِّفَ الْقُلُوْبِ صَرِّفْ
قُلُوْبَنَا عَلَى طَاعَتِكَ

O Allah! Controller of the hearts, direct our hearts to Your obedience.

Dua for increasing your knowledge

اللَّهُمَّ انْفَعْنِي بِمَا عَلَّمْتَنِي
وَعَلِّمْنِي مَا يَنْفَعُنِي وَزِدْنِي عِلْمًا

O Allah! Benefit me through what You teach me, teach me what is beneficial for me, and increase me in knowledge.

RAMADAN

1 What is your favorite hobby and why?

2 Name something new you learned this year.

3 What makes you feel peaceful?

7 What is your happiest memory?

8 What family tradition do you love the most?

9 What is your favorite animal and why?

13 Say something you appreciate about each family member.

14 What do you find most interesting about Ramadan?

15 What challenges have you overcome that you're proud of?

19 What do you admire about your siblings or friends?

20 What was the tastiest thing you ate recently?

21 Who is someone you trust and why?

25 What is your favorite weather and why?

26 Reflect on your favorite moments from the past three weeks of Ramadan

27 What name of Allah (swt) do you feel closest to and why?

Every day, find a fun question on this calendar to answer and learn something cool about yourself and the world!

4 Who is someone you look up to? Why?

5 Share a story about a time you helped someone.

6 What is your favorite book and why?

10 What do you love most about your room?

11 What is your favorite game to play?

12 What are you proud of yourself for?

16 Recall a time someone made you smile.

17 What is your favorite scent or smell?

18 What was the best part of your day today?

22 What part of the day do you look forward to most?

23 What is something about your health that you're thankful for?

24 What piece of technology are you thankful for?

28 What story or character from a book inspires you?

29 What is a talent you have that you are thankful for?

30 What sunnah of the Prophet (pbuh) do you find most inspiring?

RAMADAN MUBAR

A K
OUR SADAGAH BOX

DAY 1

TODAY'S MOOD:

DATE:

Our Prophet was known for his honesty; even his adversaries trusted him with their valuables.

"The intention of the believer is more valuable than his action."

I'M GRATEFUL FOR:

On Ramadan 1, 2 A.H., Muslims observed their first obligatory fast.

The second year after the Hijra

O Allah, guide me to always speak kindly to others.

Host a "Fav Ramadan Flashback" evening where each family member takes a turn to share their most cherished memory from the last Ramadan.

MY RAMADAN MILESTONES

- [ ] My name is
- [ ] I am years old.
- [ ] This Ramadan I want to
- [ ] My favorite food is
- [ ] My favorite thing about Ramadan is

DAY 2

TODAY'S MOOD:

DATE:

Our Prophet lived a simple life although he was the leader of all Muslims.

"Believers should show mercy to those who are young and respect the elderly."

I'M GRATEFUL FOR:

On Ramadan 2, 9 A.H., Himyarite rulers from southern Yemen accepted Islam, further spreading Islam in the region.

O Allah, help me to always be thankful for my blessings.

Become a kitchen star by helping with Iftar or Suhoor meals. You can even set a theme for the dinner table!

ALPHABET CHALLENGE

Write down things you're grateful for, beginning with each letter of the alphabet.

A

B

C

D

E

F

G

H

I

J

K

L

M

N

O

P

Q

R

S

T

U

V

W

X

Y

Z

DAY 3

TODAY'S MOOD:

DATE:

Our Prophet showed mercy to everyone and everything. He taught that we should show mercy to all, whoever they may be, and that this is a fundamental aspect of our iman.

"A believer is the mirror of another believer."

I'M GRATEFUL FOR:

O Allah, grant me the courage to stand up for what is right.

Transform into a sharing superhero and give away toys or books you no longer need to kids who would cherish them.

WINDOWS

There's a special shape that appears in two of the windows, but it's missing in the third one. Can you spot which shape it is?

PUZZLE & BUMFUZZLE

BLANK SQUARES

Pair each numbered square with a blank square.

DECODER

Crack the code! Use the pictures below to find the letters that match each image. Then, fill in the blanks in the speech bubble to reveal the secret phrase.

DAY 4

TODAY'S MOOD:

DATE:

Our Prophet showed forgiveness and goodwill even towards his foes.

"A Muslim is a person whose hands and words make everyone feel safe."

I'M GRATEFUL FOR:

On Ramadan 4, 1 A.H., the Prophet established a brotherhood between the Muhajirun (immigrants from Mecca) and the Ansar (helpers from Medina).

O Allah, help me to always be patient and understanding.

Play the role of a secret gratitude agent, leaving surprise thank-you notes for family members around the house.

IFTAR PARTY PLANNING

date & time

GUEST LIST

MENU

ACTIVITIES

GIFTS

DAY 5

TODAY'S MOOD:

DATE:

Our Prophet endured hardships and remained loyal to his mission.

"There are two blessings that people take for granted: health and spare time."

I'M GRATEFUL FOR:

O Allah, guide me to always honor my commitments.

Take on the "Extra Helpful Challenge" by doing unexpected chores around the house. See how many you can do in a week!

SWEET RAMADAN MONSTERS

Our cheerful monsters are searching for things to be grateful for. Help them discover their gratitude treasures!

DAY 6

TODAY'S MOOD:

DATE:

Our Prophet demonstrated a deep trust in Allah throughout his life.

"The key to Paradise is saying La ilaha illallah."

I'M GRATEFUL FOR:

On Ramadan 6, 6 A.H., a drought in Medina was relieved by the Prophet's prayer for rain.

O Allah, help me to be a source of comfort for my family.

Turn into a neighborhood detective and discover what special thing you can make or do for a friend or neighbor.

WEEKLY IFTAR PLANNING

Take the chef's hat and lead the way! Plan weekly iftar menu and make it a family feast to remember!

monday

---

tuesday

---

wednesday

---

thursday

---

friday

---

saturday

---

sunday

DAY 7

TODAY'S MOOD:

DATE:

Our Prophet displayed courage in the face of adversity and danger.

"Everyone makes mistakes. The best person is the one who seeks forgiveness after making a mistake."

I'M GRATEFUL FOR:

In the 10th year of the Prophethood, the beloved uncle of the Prophet, Abu Talib, passed away on Ramadan 7.

O Allah, grant me the ability to forgive others easily.

Go on a community adventure by volunteering at a local center. You might meet new friends or learn cool things!

FAST

SUHOOR QURAN TARAWIH HELP

PAPER CONE COWS

Gather your craft supplies and let's start crafting your cute cow buddy!

Grab a white paper.

Form the body by rolling the paper into a cone and secure with glue.

Trim off the excess paper.

Cut out the head, ears, tail, spots from black paper, and horns from yellow paper.

Glue the head to the top of the cone.

Use pink paper or a marker to add the nose.

Add the eyes, spots, and tail to the cone body.

Stand up your cow to display.

DAY 8

TODAY'S MOOD:

DATE:

Our Prophet was known for his just and fair treatment of others.

"Eat together and not separately, for the blessings are associated with the company."

I'M GRATEFUL FOR:

On Ramadan 8, 10 A.H., ten members of the Banu Ghamid tribe embraced Islam in Medina.

O Allah, help me to always be sincere in my actions.

Share your super skills! Teach a friend or sibling something fun and new, like a beautiful lantern craft or a Ramadan greeting card.

PUZZLE & BUMFUZZLE

LANTERNS

Spot the column that has seven unique lanterns.

CRESCENT AND STARS

Look for the one shape out of six that is not like the others.

RIDDLE

Solve the riddle on the sign by removing the letters Q, X, and Z. Then, read the remaining letters in order to find the answer.

DAY 9

TODAY'S MOOD: DATE:

Our Prophet had deep wisdom and insight.

"A kind word is charity."

I'M GRATEFUL FOR:

On Ramadan 9, 9 A.H., the Taif delegation came to Medina to meet Prophet Muhammad (pbuh) and were welcomed to stay in Masjid al-Nabawi.

O Allah, guide me to be a good listener and understand others.

Be a charity champion by organizing a clothing drive. It's like leading a treasure hunt for clothes that can help others.

FAMILY GAME NIGHT

Get ready for a fun and engaging family game night! Share laughter, insights, and make memorable moments with your loved ones. Gather around, pick a question, and dive into conversations that celebrate the spirit of Ramadan.

- What world problem would you solve during Ramadan?
- Describe your perfect Eid day from morning to night.
- Who would you share Iftar meal with and why?
- What is your dream Ramadan travel destination?
- What new Ramadan tradition would you start?
- What is your funniest and dearset Ramadan memory?
- What is the most meaningful Ramadan tradition to you?

DAY 10

TODAY'S MOOD:

DATE:

Our Prophet showed modesty in his behavior and lifestyle.

"Give gifts to each other to strengthen the friendship between you."

I'M GRATEFUL FOR:

In the 10th year of the Prophethood, Khadijah (r.anha) passed away on Ramadan 10.

O Allah, bless me with a strong memory and quick understanding.

Lead a neighborhood clean-up crew. It's like being on a secret mission to protect the environment!

FAST

SUHOOR QURAN TARAWIH HELP

NO-BAKE DATE BALLS

Take the chef's hat and lead the way! Plan weekly iftar menu and make it a family feast to remember!

1 In a food processor, combine dates and assorted nuts until sticky. Add cocoa powder and process to create a uniform mix.

2 Scoop out the mixture and roll into small balls with your hands.

3 Roll each ball in shredded coconut until well-coated.

Place the coconut balls in the refrigerator to set. Enjoy your treats after iftar!

DAY 11

TODAY'S MOOD:

DATE:

Our Prophet was known for his generosity and concern for the needy.

"A generous person is close to Allah and Paradise."

I'M GRATEFUL FOR:

On Ramadan 11, 10 A.H., the Banu Bajila tribe embraced Islam in Medina.

O Allah, help me to be brave in facing life's challenges.

Host a Virtual Story Time where you share your favorite Ramadan stories with friends online. You can even dress up as characters from the stories!

FAST

SUHOOR QURAN TARAWIH HELP

RAMADAN SCAVENGER HUNT

Are you ready to find the treasures of Ramadan?
Look around, learn, and collect memories while you enjoy the hunt.

The Holy Quran

Charity box

Prayer mat

Ramadan calendar

Date fruit

Ramadan greeting card

Ramadan decoration

Crescent moon symbol

Picture of Kaaba

Picture of a mosque

Islamic art

Traditional Ramadan food

DAY 12

TODAY'S MOOD:

DATE:

I'M GRATEFUL FOR:

Our Prophet showed kindness and gentleness in his interactions.

"If you want to live a long life filled with blessings, be kind to your parents and visit your family members."

On Ramadan 12, 2 A.H., Prophet Muhammad (pbuh) shared a camel ride with his companions, showing humility and equality.

O Allah, guide me to be respectful towards my elders.

Craft an "Acts of Kindness" Jar. Fill a jar with slips of paper, each with a different act of kindness on it, and try to do one each day.

FAST

SUHOOR QURAN TARAWIH HELP

MAKE YOUR OWN PLATE

Find out what goes into a healthy meal and put together your own delicious and nutritious dinner for iftar today!

DAY 13

TODAY'S MOOD:

DATE:

Our Prophet demonstrated empathy towards the suffering of others.

"A Muslim does not go to sleep with a full stomach while knowing that their neighbor is hungry."

I'M GRATEFUL FOR:

On Ramadan 13, 9 A.H., one of the important tribes near Medina, the Hemdan tribe, visited the Prophet and chose Islam.

O Allah, help me to be a good example for my siblings and friends.

Organize a Book Swap in your neighborhood. It's like a treasure hunt for new stories!

FAST

SUHOOR QURAN TARAWIH HELP

WEEKLY DHIKR PLANNING

Come together as a family and write down your dhikr plan for the second week of Ramadan.

MOM

DAD

ME

OTHER FAMILY MEMBERS

DAY 14

TODAY'S MOOD:

DATE:

Our Prophet advocated for the respect and fair treatment of women.

"If a person helps a believer in this world, Allah will help them in the Hereafter."

I'M GRATEFUL FOR:

O Allah, grant me the strength to avoid bad habits.

Put on a Puppet Show about Ramadan for your family or friends. You can make the puppets yourself!

LETTERS

Find the shape that includes all the letters in "CHARITY."
Note: Some letters might appear more than once.

10 DIFFERENCES

Find the 10 differences between the left and right sides of the mosque.

WHO AM I ?

Use the guidelines on the right, and figure out who I am:

- I'm not wearing striped clothing.
- I am wearing dotted clothing.
- My shoes don't have any black color.
- My pants are the same color as my shoes.
- I'm not wearing square-patterned clothing.

DAY 15

TODAY'S MOOD:

DATE:

Our Prophet showed affection and care for children.

"When you see a learning circle, join it because learning circles are like gardens of Paradise."

I'M GRATEFUL FOR:

On Ramadan 15, 3 A.H., Hasan (r.a), the grandson of the Prophet, was born.

O Allah, help me to always be grateful for my health and well-being.

Try being a "Smile Ambassador" for a day, aiming to make as many people smile as possible.

GOOD DEEDS BASKET

Ready to craft and spread kindness? Weave your very own basket and fill it with notes of good deeds!

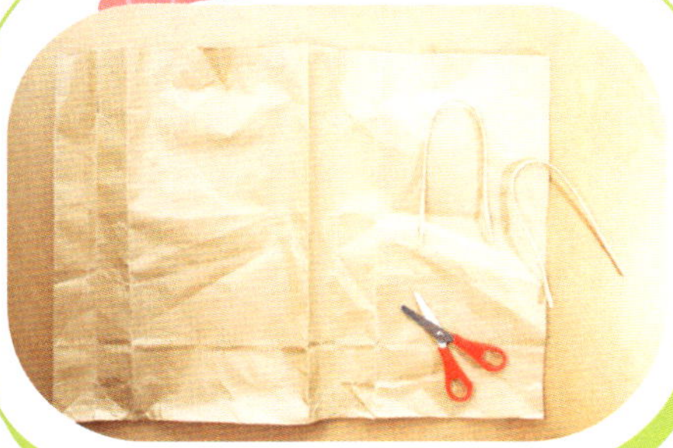

Collect brown paper, scissors, ruler, and glue.

Cut paper into strips with a ruler.

Arrange half the strips vertically.

Weave the rest horizontally and glue ends.

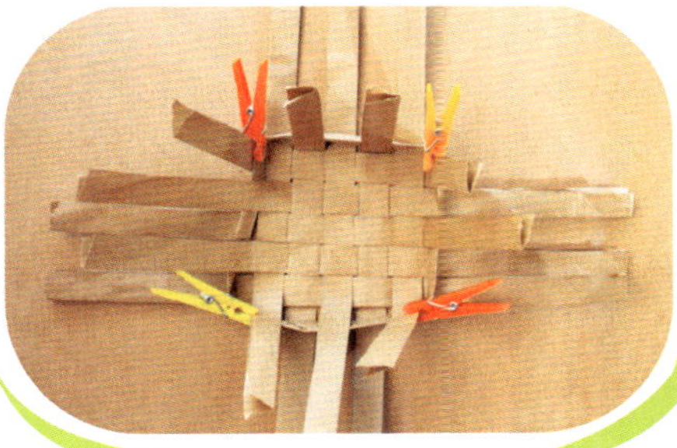

Bend vertical strips up to form sides.

Weave new strips around to make sides.

Trim excess paper at the top and glue.

Add a strip for the handle and secure.

Your "Good Deeds Basket" is ready!

DAY 16

TODAY'S MOOD:

DATE:

Our Prophet cared for the well-being of animals.

"Allah will make the path to Paradise easy for the person who seeks knowledge."

I'M GRATEFUL FOR:

On Ramadan 16, 8 A.H., our Prophet (pbuh) welcomed his relatives Abdullah Ibn Abi Umayya and Abu Sufyan Ibn Haris into Islam.

O Allah, guide me to be conscious of my time and use it wisely.

Make "Blessing Bags" with essentials and a kind note, and give them to those in need.

VLOG A DAY IN RAMADAN

Grab your camera and bring your Ramadan days to life for the world to see! Check out these fun vlog ideas to share your experiences during this holy month.

1. Showcase your homemade Ramadan decorations or crafts.
2. Capture the less-seen moments of Ramadan.
3. Share a meaningful story or lesson you learned during the day.

4. Explore how Ramadan is celebrated in different cultures.
5. Create time-lapses of your Iftar preparations.
6. Chat with family members about their Ramadan experiences.

7. Highlight local community events or charity initiatives.
8. Turn your Iftar meals into artful presentations and share tips.
9. Share snippets from your gratitude journal.

DAY 17

TODAY'S MOOD:

DATE:

Our Prophet exhibited a deep spiritual connection and devotion.

"The daily prayers are the best deed."

I'M GRATEFUL FOR:

On 17 Ramadan 610, the Quran started being revealed to our beloved Prophet in the Hira cave on Mount Nur.

O Allah, bless me with the ability to help those in need.

Set up a bird oasis by putting out water and birdseed in your yard or balcony.

RAMADAN BINGO

Mark off all the items in a row, column, or diagonal to complete the game!

Help clean after iftar	Cook a traditional Ramadan dish	Call or visit grandparents	Volunteer at a local charity
Give charity to a needy person	Read Quran for 15 minutes	Do a random act of kindness	Perform at least two Salat on time
Attend Tarawih prayer	Share Ramadan knowledge with a friend	Wake up for Fajr prayer	Reflect on your personal goals for Ramadan
Learn about the history of Eid al-Fitr	Listen to a Ramadan-themed song	Learn a new Surah and recite it	Take some extra time for dua

DAY 18

TODAY'S MOOD:

DATE:

Our Prophet had exceptional leadership qualities.

"If anyone invokes blessings upon me once, Allah will bestow blessings upon them ten times over."

I'M GRATEFUL FOR:

In the first year of the Prophethood, Ali (r.a) and Zayd ibn Haritha (r.a) chose Islam on Ramadan 18.

O Allah, help me to maintain purity in thought and action.

Write a Ramadan Poem and share it with your family during Iftar.

REFLECTION

Spot 10 differences between the picture and its reflection.

ARRANGE

Reorder the words from 1 to 8 to correctly read the hadith.

MAKE A WORD

Rearrange the picture parts 1 to 9 from left to right, then write the corresponding letters in the boxes below in this order.

1 2 3 4 5 6 7 8 9

DAY 19

TODAY'S MOOD:

DATE:

Our Prophet forgave people, even if they weren't nice to him. He taught us to be friends and make peace with everyone.

"Treat people with kindness."

I'M GRATEFUL FOR:

On Ramadan 19, 8 A.H., Mecca was peacefully conquered by the Prophet (pbuh).

O Allah, guide me to be a peacemaker and spread harmony.

Plant a tree in your community or garden as a symbol of growth and giving back to the environment.

RAMADAN GARDEN

An indoor plant is a beautiful way to see how patience and care can help something grow, just like our good deeds in Ramadan. Grab a pot and some seeds!

1. A small pot or container.
2. Potting soil.
3. Indoor plant seeds (herbs or small flowers).
4. Watering can or spray bottle.
5. Plant label for naming.

Choose a Seed: Pick an indoor-friendly seed like herbs or small flowers.

Prepare the Pot: Fill it with soil and plant your seeds just below the surface.

Name Your Plant: Write a fun name on the label and place it in the soil.

Find a Sunny Spot: Place your pot somewhere with indirect sunlight.

Water and Watch: Use a spray bottle to keep the soil moist. Watch for sprouts!

Journal Your Journey: Write or draw in your Ramadan Journal about your plant's growth and your thoughts.

DAY 20

TODAY'S MOOD:

DATE:

Our Prophet remained humble despite his successes.

"Tie your camel safely and then trust it in Allah's care."

I'M GRATEFUL FOR:

On Ramadan 20, 3 A.H., our Prophet (pbuh) started his first I'tikaf.

O Allah, help me to be mindful of my duties and responsibilities.

Lead a family exercise session. Keeping healthy is important during Ramadan!

WEEKLY ACTS OF KINDNESS CHALLENGE

Sit with your family and think of kind things you can do each day.
At the end of the week, share your experiences with each other.

monday

tuesday

wednesday

thursday

friday

saturday

sunday

DAY 21

TODAY'S MOOD:

DATE:

Our Prophet respected and valued diversity among people.

"Muslims are brothers and sisters to one another. They do not harm one another or let others harm their fellow Muslims."

I'M GRATEFUL FOR:

On Ramadan 21, 2 A.H., on the journey from Badr to Medina, our Prophet (pbuh) advised Muslims to treat their captives kindly.

O Allah, bless me with the ability to adapt and learn from every situation.

Be a "Water Wizard" by reminding everyone to drink water at Suhoor to stay hydrated.

MY DUA LIST FOR THE LAST TEN DAYS

As the last 10 days of Ramadan arrive, make a list of all the things you want to ask Allah for during this super special time!

DAY 22

TODAY'S MOOD:

DATE:

Our Prophet upheld truthfulness in all aspects of life.

"Do not harm others, even if you are harmed first."

I'M GRATEFUL FOR:

On Ramadan 22, 3 A.H., the Prophet held an "Aqiqah" ceremony for his grandson Hasan, on the 7th day after his birth.

O Allah, guide me to be appreciative of others' efforts towards me.

Start a Gratitude Chain by adding a link each day with something you're thankful for.

FAST

SUHOOR QURAN TARAWIH HELP

COLOR MY RAMADAN T-SHIRT

Imagine a T-shirt that tells your unique Ramadan story. Each stroke of color brings your Ramadan experiences to life!

DAY 23

TODAY'S MOOD:

DATE:

Our Prophet was devoted to prayer and ibadah.

"Allah is pleased with people who complete their work and do it well."

I'M GRATEFUL FOR:

On Ramadan 23, 2 A.H., Ruqayyah (r.anha), the Prophet's daughter, passed away.

O Allah, help me to be a source of positive energy in my community.

Make iftar invitations for your family, even if you're just eating at home. It makes your iftar extra special!

WORD SEARCH

Search for words related to zakat that Zahra read about, hidden among the letters in the table. Look up, down, forward, and diagonally to find them.

PUZZLE & BUMFUZZLE

BLESSING
DONATE
SADAQAH
SOLIDARITY
PURIFY
NISAB
NEEDY
RAMADAN
PILLAR

P	B	N	X	I	W	B	Y	L	V	J	D	R	J
B	L	G	S	B	L	F	A	C	E	O	W	A	Q
R	E	M	T	A	I	G	Z	S	N	L	K	L	E
W	S	Y	E	R	D	Q	W	A	I	H	L	L	G
G	S	O	U	K	K	A	T	I	F	N	L	I	C
B	I	P	H	F	A	E	Q	S	D	Q	I	P	H
O	N	Y	D	E	E	N	R	A	M	A	D	A	N
G	G	O	H	Z	L	E	C	N	H	V	O	L	Q
N	Y	T	I	R	A	D	I	L	O	S	Q	X	I

MATCH

Pair each lectern with the right child.

DAY 24

TODAY'S MOOD:

DATE:

Our Prophet showed special compassion for the poor and underprivileged.

"Patience is half of faith."

I'M GRATEFUL FOR:

On Ramadan 24, 8 A.H., the Prophet sent Khalid Ibn Al-Walid (r.a) with a group to destroy the Uzza idol, a big idol near Mecca.

O Allah, grant me the wisdom to make the right choices in life.

Be a "No Complaints Ninja" for a day - try to go all day without complaining.

SPARKLY CRESCENT MOON

Sparkle up some magic with glitter and cardbox to make a shiny crescent moon!

1 Cut a 2-inch wide cardboard strip, fold it, and glue the edges.

2 Form the strip into a crescent shape.

3 Flatten the toilet paper roll and cut into strips.

4 Glue the leaves inside the cardboard crescent.

5 Sprinkle glitter over the crescent. Allow to dry for your sparkly moon.

DAY 25

TODAY'S MOOD:

DATE:

I'M GRATEFUL FOR:

Our Prophet demonstrated resilience in overcoming challenges.

"Allah treats people with compassion, so He loves people being compassionate with one another."

In the first year of the Prophethood, the family of Jahsh chose Islam on Ramadan 25. They were among the first Muslims.

O Allah, help me to be patient in achieving my goals.

Put on an indoor play about a story from the Quran or Seerah.

FAST

SUHOOR QURAN TARAWIH HELP

OVERNIGHT OATS FOR SUHOOR

1

In a jar, pour your desired amount of oats. Add yogurt or milk to the oats until they are well submerged.

2

Drizzle honey or your choice of sweetener on top. Stir the mixture to combine all the ingredients.

3

Close the jar and refrigerate overnight. The next suhoor, top your oats with fresh fruits and enjoy!

DAY 26

TODAY'S MOOD:

DATE:

Our Prophet was committed to teaching and guiding others.

"There are three prayers that are always accepted: the prayer of the oppressed, the prayer of the traveler, and the prayer of the parents."

I'M GRATEFUL FOR:

On Ramadan 26, 5 A.H., the Surah An-Nur was revealed.

O Allah, guide me to be a caring and loving individual.

Become a "Neighborhood Nature Protector" by picking up litter during your walks.

MY PLANS FOR EID

MY TOP GOAL:

EID PRESENTS I'M WISHING FOR:

1

2

3

4

5

I'D LIKE TO WEAR:

I'D LIKE TO EAT AND DRINK:

I WOULD LIKE TO DO:

DAY 27

TODAY'S MOOD:

DATE:

Our Prophet showed patience during times of adversity.

"If a person causes a good deed to be done, they will be rewarded as if they had performed the good deed themselves."

I'M GRATEFUL FOR:

On Ramadan 27, 10 A.H., the Prophet recited the Quran to Jibril for the last time.

O Allah, bless me with the ability to overcome fear and anxiety.

Start a "Gratitude Roundtable" 10 minutes before Iftar. Everyone gets a turn to share one thing they're grateful for that day.

FAST

SUHOOR QURAN TARAWIH HELP

LAYLAT-UL QADR

THE NIGHT OF POWER

The Quran was revealed to our Prophet (saw) on Laylat-ul Qadr!

DUA FOR LAYLAT-UL QADR

Allahumma innaka `afuwwun tuhibbul `afwa fa`fu `annee'.

O Allah, You are the Most Forgiving and You love to forgive, so forgive me.

Your 1 good deed on this night is worth 1000 MONTHS OF REWARD

The exact date of Laylat-ul Qadr is not known, which makes it even more special. We should seek it in the last ten nights of Ramadan, especially the odd-numbered ones.

DO DHIKR AND MAKE DUA!

Allah says in the Quran, "Laylat-ul Qadr is better than a thousand months."

DAY 28

TODAY'S MOOD:

DATE:

Our Prophet expressed gratitude in all circumstances.

"Believers are like a firm and solid structure."

I'M GRATEFUL FOR:

On Ramadan 28, 2 A.H., Sadaqat al-Fitr became obligatory. It's a way to thank Allah and help others.

O Allah, help me to always trust in Your plan and timing.

Embark on a "Salawat Challenge" today: say 100 Salawat!

RAMADAN TIME CAPSULE

Grab your art gear and a box of dreams-we're diving into a Ramadan adventure! Doodle, scribble, and stash your precious Ramadan moments in a capsule.

Pen down your thoughts from this Ramadan the stories, the lessons, and the laughs. Add your duas, too! What do you hope for yourself and your loved ones in the next year? Let every word be a seed for the future.

Now, seal your capsule with joy and a promise of reunion. Label it with a big "See you next Ramadan!" Imagine the excitement when you uncover the treasures next year!

DAY 29

TODAY'S MOOD:

DATE:

Our Prophet encouraged people to increase their knowledge.

"The most beloved deeds to Allah are the ones that are continuous, even if they are little."

I'M GRATEFUL FOR:

In the first year of the Prophethood, Amr Ibn Abasa (r.a) became a Muslim on Ramadan 29.

O Allah, guide me to be diligent and hardworking in all my endeavors.

Attend the Tarawih prayer and pray for all people in need.

EID SUNNAHS

Before going to Eid prayer, take a shower (ghusl) to make sure you are clean and ready for the special day.

Eat something sweet before going to prayer.

Try to go to the Eid prayer early.

Wear your best clothes.

When leaving for the prayer, say "Allahu Akbar," which means "God is the greatest."

Say "Eid Mubarak" to your friends and family, which means "Happy Eid."

Visit your relatives and friends.

Thank Allah for giving you the ability to fast and complete the month of Ramadan!

DAY 30

TODAY'S MOOD:

DATE:

Our Prophet embraced inclusivity in his teachings and actions.

"Do good deeds after you sin so that Allah may forgive your sins."

I'M GRATEFUL FOR:

Host a "Moon Gazing Night!" Spend an evening with family or friends gazing at the moon, sharing thoughts and stories about Ramadan and hopes for the year ahead.

O Allah, help me to be conscious of You in all my actions and thoughts.

Yay! You did it!

Alhamdulillah, you've come to the end of Ramadan and this Ramadan journal.

Put your photos (or draw pictures) of your favorite moments from Ramadan and Eid!

toward parents.	right side.	hand for eating and drinking.	Ikhlas, Falaq, and An-Nas before bed.	food that is too hot.
Perform acts of kindness for neighbors.	Assist in household chores.	Share kind words, food, and gifts.	Eat what is in front of you first.	Do not blow on the food; let it cool down naturally.
Recite the dua for eating together.	Chew food properly without talking.	Take only as much food as you can eat.	Avoid wasting food.	Express love and affection to parents.
Say Alhamdulillah after eating and drinking.	Say Bismillah and Salaam when entering the house.	Drink water in three sips, not in one gulp.	Make wudhu before sleeping at night.	**HAPPY EID!**

ATLASIA KIDS

Discover the Prophet's Sunnahs that brighten each night of Ramadan! Every day, cut open a window on the starry night page and discover a Sunnah. Like stars in the sky, these daily Sunnahs will guide and inspire you through this holy month.

Begin actions with Bismillah.	**Greet others with respect and a smile.**	**Use the best speech and kind words.**	**Speak the truth.**	**Admit and own up to mistakes.**
Dust the bed before getting into it.	**Recite dua before sleeping.**	**Respect the rights of neighbors.**	**Be a good friend.**	**Eat and drink while sitting down.**
		Use the right	**Recite Surah**	

11
12
13
14
15
16
17
18
19
20
21
22
23
24
25
26
27
28
29
30

A SUNNAH A DAY

1	2	3	4	5
6	7	8	9	10

AHMANIRRAHIM

* Eat with your **right hand** and say **Alhamdulillah** after your meal!

BISMILLAHIRR

Dua for breaking fast

Thirst has gone, the veins are moist, and the reward is assured, if Allah wills.

Dua after eating

All praise is to Allah who gave us food and drink and who made us Muslims.

Dear .... family

You're invited to our

iFTAR PARTY

date: ....

time: ....

address: ....

RAMADAN KAREEM

Dear .... family

You're invited to our

iFTAR PARTY

date: ....

time: ....

address: ....

RAMADAN KAREEM

Dear .... family

You're invited to our

iFTAR PARTY

date: ....

time: ....

address: ....

RAMADAN KAREEM

Dear .... family

You're invited to our

iFTAR PARTY

date: ....

time: ....

address: ....

RAMADAN KAREEM